North East Men
东北人

Photography / 摄影
Wang Fuchun 王福春

Foreword by Li Zhensheng (*)
Wang Fuchun: from black land to world stage

From one kind of earth grows one kind of man, Wang Fuchun was born and grew up in the black land. This land will always be his spiritual home. Born in 1943 in the Suihua County of the Heilongjiang province, Wang Fuchun is the typical Northeast man. Through unremitting endeavor and untiring efforts, he walked out of the black land and traveled all around the country. Since, he has also walked onto the world stage.

In 1963 after my graduation I worked as a photojournalist at the Heilongjiang Daily News in Harbin, the same icy cold northern city as Wang Fuchun's. In those days the press had to follow Chairman Mao's instruction that "newspaper is made with the help of everybody, with the help of all the people..." therefore, news of a province paper relied on the reports from correspondents at the city and county levels. At first I was in charge of communication and liaison then in 1972 as photo editor I had more occasions to come into contact with other professional or amateur photographers of various local papers. I also had the chance to edit the pictures of some of them who later became famous photographers in a document called "my first photos published in the Heilongjiang Daily News." These include Xu Lishun of the Daxinanling Forest Area and those from the Heilongjiang production and construction corps such as Zhou Que, Shi Zhimin, and Huang Chengjiang and so on. I had heard of someone named Wang Fuchun who was involved in art propaganda at the Hatie Steel Factory and who was also practicing photography, but until I left the Heilongjiang Daily in 1982 I never had a chance to come across any of his pictures; that was something I always regretted. Later I asked Fuchun why he did not submit any photo to the province paper, he said: "In those days it was a glorious thing to be published in the province paper, as an amateur photographer I did not dare knock on the paper's door." One can see in his humbleness Wang Fuchun was already someone with character and potential.

By 1996 at the occasion of the 30th anniversary of the Cultural Revolution, the then Editor in Chief of Hong Kong's M photo agency Liu Heungshing and a reporter of Germany's Stern Weekly came to interview me in Beijing. They wanted me to take them to Harbin in search of some of the people who appeared in my old Cultural Revolution series. Before we left Beijing I telephoned some old friends such as Wang Fuchun so that after all these years we could meet again for a chat at the Garden state guesthouse. Knowing Wang Fuchun's documentary photography I especially introduced him to Liu. Together we reviewed Wang's works which left a deep impression on Liu Heungshing. As a result Wang's photographs were published in different international magazines. Even the title of "Chinese on the Train" was given by Liu himself. Later on at the request of Liu Heungshing, Wang Fuchun has diligently realized a series of portraits of the Northeast people in a snow white setting. In the meantime Wang Fuchun's "Chinese on the Train" was published by Le Monde 2 and exhibited in a Paris gallery. Over the years his exhibition was shown successively in Denmark, Russia, USA, France, Holland etc and received high praise. Wang Fuchun's photography has finally risen beyond Asia and reached the world stage.

In April 1998 thirty years after I photographed "the loyalist," I wrote an article in the China Southern Weekly magazine titled "Wang Guoxiang where are you?" which quickly led to an answer. The Harbin TV station invited me back to Heilongjiang to meet with the "loyalist", and my old friend Wang Fuchun accompanied me all the way on the train to Tsitsihar to document our historical reunion.

The black land has always been the foundation of Wang Fuchun's photographic creation, where he produced a great quantity of portraits of the Northeast people with excellent results. After winning his Best Photography Book Award for "Chinese on the Train" at the 2002 Pingyao Festival, in 2004 he won the Pingyao Grand Prix for Best Chinese Contemporary Photographer with his "Northeast People." Then at Jinan's International Biennale he received the highest Academic Award in 2006 and again in 2008 he won the PPA Most Outstanding Photographer Award with his "Black Land."

In recent years I have often been traveling with Robert Pledge (*) to various photography events in China. In October 2004 while we participated to the Forbidden City Photo Festival, I introduced Wang Fuchun to Pledge, who looked at his pictures with great interest and appreciation. They have become good friends; each time they meet in Beijing or Pingyao they hug each other warmly and affectionately.

Over the years Wang Fuchun remains deeply attached to his homeland of Heilongjiang, unaffected by success or fame or by the calls of bright cities and foreign lands. His gaze has always been fixated on his beloved black earth country, his camera pointed at his home land folks. Though I am three years older than Fuchun, we belong to the same generation and both we have reached the age of playing with grandsons. Yet neither of us will let go of the camera. What sets us apart is: the camera I use is getting smaller and smaller, passing from analog to digital; whereas Fuchun's camera is getting bigger and bigger, from 120 medium format to 8x10 large format and he is still hanging onto traditional negative film. Whereas my custom is to photograph randomly as I travel, Wang Fuchun always creates according to a theme or a topic.

Wang Fuchun has carried his 8x10 view camera through his journey in the black land, braving cold wind and treading thick snow, sleeping outdoor, with mountains climbed and rivers crossed he worked hard during three winters to achieve his creative masterpiece. Like he said "I am an authentic Northeast man; the black land is the fertile soil where I grew up, the mountains and rivers of this country of cockscomb shape are forever engraved in my heart." As an old friend of his I really admire Fuchun's unyielding energy in artistic creation, his strong will and unwavering pursuit, and his the-older-you-grow-the-more-you-learn attitude.

It was through Wang Fuchun's introduction that I met international curator Jean Loh at the 2003 Pingyao Festival. We became good friends at once and share our common passion for photography ever since. Now Jean is to curate Wang Fuchun's "Northeast Men" exhibition in Shanghai, with a catalogue of the same title; he has kindly invited me to write a preface, and as Fuchun's old buddy I can only dutifully comply and here is my contribution with this rambling foreword.

Li Zhensheng
At my Wuwei Studio in New York

18th of December 2008

(*) Editor's notes:
Li Zhensheng (b.1940), China's master of photography, his famous exhibition RED COLOR NEWS SOLDIER is still touring museums around the world since 2003.
Robert Pledge (b.1942), founded Contact Press in New York with David Burnett in 1975, world class curator and co-author with Li Zhensheng of the award winning book RED COLOR NEWS SOLDIER.

* Editor's notes:
"BLACK LAND" – Wang Fuchun B&W photography, 40p, printed by Shenzhen Dexinmei Ltd, first edition 2002.
"CHINESE ON THE TRAIN" – Wang Fuchun B&W photography, 120p, Heilongjiang Art Publishing House, first edition 2001. Winner of Alcatel Best Chinese Photography Book Award at 2002 Pingyao Photo Festival – the title was given by Liu Heungshing

Seasons Greetings from the Northeast Men

Born in the country of Black Land (hei tudi*), Wang Fuchun has two loves: one is the railroad, with its steam locomotives and its "Chinese on the train" he so often encounters; the other his own countrymen of the Northeast (Dong Bei Ren). On both subjects Wang has established and proven his reputation as one of the best documentary photographers in China.

This series of "Northeast Men" photographs, exhibited here for the first time in Shanghai, is like Wang Fuchun himself: authentic and natural, honest and straightforward, ever optimistic and with a warm, big heart as pure as an ice crystal.

The first impression might well be a bowl of fresh air thrown in our faces: his portraits of the Northeast Men appear to depict a paradise on earth, where animals and men look just as they have always been, since the oldest ages, living in peace and harmony, with the environment in pristine condition. In that sense Wang Fuchun's photography should be classified as an endangered species, threatened by extinction. Only in our deepest collective unconscious minds could we have dreamed of such a perfect world where, according to the Daoist principle, Heaven, Man and Earth are set in a circular, balanced, perpetual interaction, yet at the same time with a permanence that is supposed to last for eternity.

There is not a single individual portrait to be found. The Northeast Men appear either in families or in couples as if in the great cold Northern country solitude is by nature forbidden, which explains the energy, warmth, sense of friendship, solidarity and fierce loyalty well known among the Dong Bei Ren, and winningly demonstrated in the group portrait of the winter swimmers on ice, revealing plenty of skin as well as camaraderie. There is no urban hassle, no pollution, no financial meltdown, no god's warriors in this "White Land" of Wang Fuchun's. It is a completely stress-free, pure and innocent world, filled with image d'Épinal, the sort of farmers' new year paintings, the kind of too-real-to-be-true folk art that reminds us of our original Garden of Eden, where we are always welcomed by our neighbors with whom we share the festive banquets, where animals, birds and fish are man's best friends.

We should all be grateful to Wang Fuchun for achieving these extraordinary folk paintings, carrying his heavy, large-format view camera and equipment, guiding us to his home country, sharing with us the love he has for his countrymen, the hospitality of his brothers and sisters, uncles and aunts, even the seldom seen Northeast ethnic minorities, the simple but abundant meals, and, most importantly, his warm heart and his pure and smiling eyes.

Let's be grateful for receiving his greeting cards for the New Year.
They give us a lesson in the rewards of optimism and also impart vital energy that should prove indispensable for overcoming the many challenges of the new year ahead.

Jean Loh
Curator
Shanghai December 2008

王福春：从黑土地走向全国并走向世界的中国摄影家

一方水土养一方人，黑土地养育了王福春。他是生于斯长于斯的一位摄影家。黑土地成为他永远的精神家园。1943年王福春出生于黑龙江省绥化县，他是一位地道的东北汉子。他凭着自己不懈的努力，终于从黑土地走了出来，走向了全国，并走向了世界。

1963年，我大学毕业后到黑龙江日报社做摄影记者，与王福春同在哈尔滨这座北方冰城工作生活。在那一段岁月里，新闻界遵照毛泽东提出的"我们的报纸要靠大家来办，靠全体人民群众来办……"的指示，省报的地方新闻稿件主要靠各地、市、县等基层单位的通讯员来稿。最初，我在摄影组负责通联工作，1972年担任摄影组长，负责编辑签发通讯员的照片稿件供报纸采用，有机会广泛接触并熟知省内各地市县报的专业摄影记者和基层的半专业或非专业摄影者，曾为几位后来成为著名摄影家的人编发"平生第一次在黑龙江日报发表图片"的记录，诸如当时在大兴安岭林区的徐力群（已故），在黑龙江生产建设兵团的周确、石志民、黄成江等等。那时，曾听说哈铁三棵树车辆段有一位以搞美术宣传为主，也兼搞摄影的王福春，直到1982年我调离黑龙江日报社到北京为止，始终没有看到他寄来的照片稿件，这成为我的一个不大不小的遗憾。后来，我问福春当年为何不向省报供稿，他说："那时能在省报上发表照片是很荣耀的事，我作为摄影爱好者还不敢登省报的大门呢"。由此可见，王福春是很有个性的人，大有引而不发，一鸣惊人之势。

1996年，适逢"文革"三十周年，时任香港M图片社总监兼《中》杂志总编辑的刘香成，与德国《星》周刊记者到北京对我作访谈，他们邀请我一起到哈尔滨追踪采访我拍摄的"文革"老照片的主人公，从北京出发之前我电话知会王福春等老朋友，我们几位老友阔别多年后又在花园村国宾馆喜相逢了。我知道王福春一直在搞纪实摄影，特地把他介绍给刘香成先生，我们一起看过他的包括火车众生相在内的几组图片，刘先生对他的纪实影像留下深刻印象，他的两组纪实摄影专题很快在《中》月刊及国际专业刊物大篇幅发表，他的《火车上的中国人》还是刘香成为其命名的。后来，刘香成又约请他拍摄一组白背景的东北人肖像，聪颖勤奋的王福春很快完成了约稿。在此期间，旅居巴黎的尚陆先生推介王福春的《火车上的中国人》在巴黎慧眼画廊展出，并在法国最大的日报《世界报》上发表。近年来陆续在丹麦、法国、俄罗斯、美国、荷兰等国家展出，广受好评，使王福春的作品"冲出亚洲，走向世界"。

1998年4月，适逢我的"文革"老照片《虔诚者》拍摄30周年，《南方周末》发表我写的《王国祥，你在哪里？》的文章，不出一个月便找到了。哈尔滨电视台邀请我重返黑龙江去追踪采访《虔诚者》的主人公王国祥，王福春作为我的老朋友同乘火车前往齐齐哈尔，为我们的历史性会面作全程记录。

王福春以家乡黑土地为摄影创作基地，大量的东北人肖像作品不断问世，连创佳绩。2002年，他的《火车上的中国人》在平遥国际摄影大展中首夺摄影画册大奖；2004年《东北人家》又在平遥荣获中国摄影师大奖。2006年又在济南国际双年展获最高学院大奖，2008年《黑土地》再次在济南国际摄影双年展荣获ppa世界职业杰出摄影师奖。

近些年来，我经常与罗伯特.普雷基一起到中国参加各类影事活动，早在2004年10月，我们参加故宫举办的"紫禁城国际摄影大展"期间，在我们下榻的宾馆内，我介绍普雷基与王福春相识，并一起看过他的很多照片，普雷基很欣赏他的纪实摄影作品。他们之间也成为好朋友，自此以后每次在北京或平遥相见都会热情拥抱，互致问候。

几十年来，王福春对黑龙江那一片沃土不弃不离，从不舍近求远地奔赴名山大川，涉猎异域民族风情，他的视野始终盯住他执爱的那一片黑土地，他的镜头一直是对准东北的父老乡亲，用"咬定黑土不放松"来形容他对家乡的依恋深情，是恰如其分的。

我比福春年长三岁，我们俩同属一个年龄段，如今都是年逾花甲直奔古稀的人了，本已到了含饴弄孙，享清福的时候。但是，我们俩仍是手不离相机，所不同的是我使用的相机越变越小，由胶片机改为数码机；福春的相机却是越来越大，从120机改为8×10大画幅相机，还始终坚持使用传统胶片拍摄。在拍摄题材上我们俩也有不同，我是走马观花随意拍摄；福春是自定选题执意创作。

王福春背着8×10大画幅相机游走在黑土地上，沿着黑龙江边境，迎着寒风，踏着积雪，风餐露宿，艰难跋涉，悉心创作，历时三冬。用他自己的话说，"我是地地道道的东北人，黑土地是我成长的沃土，那鸡冠型版图上的山山水水，是我心中永远的牵挂。"

作为老朋友，我欣佩福春在艺术创作上坚忍不拔的精神、百折不回的意志、顽强执著的追求、活到老学到老的人生态度。我相信福春的艺术青春将会长驻。

我与国际策展人尚陆先生相识于2003年的平遥大展期间，那还是王福春为我们引荐的，自那以后，我们也成了同道好友。这次尚陆先生策划王福春的"东北人"在上海展出，同时编辑出版同名画册。尚陆先生发函请我为画册作序，作为福春的老朋友，尊敬不如从命，我便写下这段不成其为序的序言。

2008年12月18日于纽约无为斋

编者注：
李振盛：中国摄影大师，他的"让历史告诉未来 – 红色新闻兵"的环球影展从2003年到现在还在世界不同国家展出。
罗伯特.普雷基：美国联系图片社创办人，与李振盛合作编辑的"红色新闻兵"画册荣获美国"欧利维尔•罗博"奖。

10

东北人的贺年卡

出生在《黑土地》的王福春一生中仅有两个喜好，一个是铁路，其上行驶的蒸汽机车和他常常邂逅的的《火车上的中国人》，其外就是他的同乡东北人。在这两个主题上王福春多年来已成功地建立并巩固了他作为中国最优秀的纪实摄影家之一的声誉。

这次在上海首展的"东北人"影像跟他自己一样：地道而自然，诚实而坦率，乐观开朗并拥有一个温暖开阔，象冰晶一样纯净的心灵。

这些影像给我们第一印象如同扑面而来的新鲜空气：他的东北人系列仿佛在描述人间天堂，野物和人类看起来好像从古至今都一直未有改变，一直平静而和谐地生活在质朴的环境和条件中。从这个角度来讲，我们应该把王福春的摄影列为濒临灭绝的一个物种。

只有在最深刻的集体无意识里，我们才可能梦想到这么一个完美的世界：天、地、人，根据道家原则，相互作用，彼此制衡，往复循环，生生不息，直至永恒。

这里没有一张单人肖像，东北人总是以家庭或夫妻的形象出现，仿佛在这个冰封雪冻的北国里，孤独是根本不被允许的。正是那组自豪的在冰上展示自己的冬浴裸者群像，淋漓尽致地展示了东北人出名的能量、热情、团结、对友情的看重及其引以为豪的忠诚。在王福春所表现的这个"白土地"里，没有都市的喧嚣，没有污染，没有金融危机，也没有为神灵而战的斗士。这是一个纯净无邪，完全除却了紧张与不安的世界。就像农民过年时候张贴的年画，亦或美好得有些不真实的民间艺术，让我们想起伊甸园的景象：邻居总会热情邀请我们来分享节日的盛宴；动物、鸟和鱼都是人类的最好的朋友。

我们应该感谢王福春，感谢他创造了这组非凡的民俗画卷，感谢他带着大型相机和设备，带我们来到他的故乡，与我们分享他对同乡的爱，他兄弟姐妹、叔叔婶婶的好客和简单但丰盛的饭食，还有更重要的，就是他温暖的心灵与带着笑意的纯净双眼。让我们为这些新年的祝福卡片表示感谢，它们带来的是为战胜未来挑战不可或缺的乐观与力量。

尚陆
策展人
Shanghai Dec 2008

*1: 《黑土地》深圳德信美印刷公司，40页，黑白摄影，2002年第一版，王福春自费画册。
*2: 《火车上的中国人》黑龙江美术出版社，120页，黑白摄影，2001年第一版。2002年平遥摄影节"阿尔卡特"最佳摄影丛书大奖。刘香成帮他起的书题。

14 冬季的雾凇人家　　　　　　　　2006吉林雾凇岛
    Happy family in winter frost and mist　　2006 Frost Mist Island Jilin

16 冰天雪地成了"天然冰箱" 2005年黑龙江双丰林场
The "natural refrigerator" 2005 Shuangfeng Forest Plantation Heilongjiang

18 杀年猪过大年 2005年黑龙江双丰林场
The new year pig for the holiday banquet 2005 Shuangfeng Forest Plantation Heilongjiang

20 远离现代文明，深居原始森林的最后的鄂伦春狩猎部落，最后一户狩猎人　　　　2005年黑龙江大兴安岭
   Far away from civilization, the last Oroqen hunting tribe living in the woods　　2005 Daxinanling forest

22 黑龙江开江捕鱼的赫哲族人家　　2006年黑龙江扶远
The Hoche fishermen　　2006 Fuyuan County Heilongjiang

24 扎龙自然保护区养鹤人家 2006年黑龙江齐齐哈尔
Crane breeding family in Zaron's nature preservation park 2006 Tsitsihar Heilongjiang

26 东北大秧歌 2005年黑龙江鸡西
The Northeast Rice Harvest Folk Dance 2005 Jixi Heilongjiang

28 不愿到城市定居，重返大山的鄂温克驯鹿人　　　　　2005年黑龙江大兴安岭
The reindeer breeding Ewenki people who refuse to live in the city　2005 Daxinanling forest

30 滑雪的山里孩子 2007年黑龙讧双丰林场
Mountain children enjoying ski 2007 Shuangfeng Forest Plantation Heilongjiang

32 最后的达斡尔族狩猎人 2006年黑龙江齐齐哈尔
The last Daur ethnic hunters 2006 Tsitsihar Heilongjiang

34 鄂伦春人祈求富贵，祈祷平安的萨满舞　　2005年黑龙江大兴安岭
Oroqen people's Shamanic dance　　2005 Daxinganling Heilongjiang

36　满族村老太太大烟袋　　　　　　　　2006年吉林韩屯
　　Long pipe grand-ma's of the Manchu village　　2006 the Han clan hamlet Jilin

38 额尔古纳河畔的华俄后裔 2005年内蒙古恩和
Russian ethnic descendants by the Argun river 2005 Enhe Inner Mongolia at the Russian border

40 为开发北大荒，献了青春献子孙， 献了子孙献终身的十万转业官兵一家人　　2005年黑龙江哈尔滨
Those officers who sacrificed their youth for the Northeast development　　2005 Ha'erbing Heilongjiang

42 朝鲜族人家　　　　　2007年吉林延边
　　Korean ethnic family　2007 Jilin Yanbian

44 呼伦贝尔草原上的"布力亚特人" 2005年呼伦贝尔草原
The Buryat people from the Hulunbeir steppe 2005 Hulunbeir steppe

46　兴凯湖冬季破冰捕鱼　　　　　2005黑龙江兴凯湖
　　Winter ice fishing in Lake Xingkai　2005 Xingkai Lake Heilongjiang

48 大山里的养狍人家 2005年黑龙江双丰林场
The deer breeding family in the mountain 2005 Shuangfeng Forest Plantation Heilongjiang

50 触入黑土地没有返城的上海知青 2005年黑龙江856农场
Shanghai zhiqing who had never returned home 2005 Farm number 856 Heilongjiang

| 54 | 冰天雪地里的冬泳人 | 2007年黑龙江双丰林场 |
| | Winter swimmers in icy snow land | 2007 Shuangfeng Forest Plantation Heilongjiang |

56 坐着马车走村串屯的东北大秧歌队 2007年黑龙江双丰林场
The Northeast Rice Harvest performers going from village to village 2007 Shuangfeng Forest Plantation Heilongjiang

58 大雪封山，人马寸步难行　　2007年黑龙讧双丰林场
Men and horses in snow-trapped mountain　　2007 Shuangfeng Forest Plantation Heilongjiang

中国最北部北极村最北一家人
The farthest household in China's Northern border at the Artic Village

2006年黑龙江摸河
2006 Mohe river Heilongjiang

62 当年到北大荒"劳动改造"至今没返城的北大荒人　　2006兴凯湖农场
Those who were sent to Northern wilderness for re-education through labor and never went home (at the farm of Xingkai Lake)

64 大山里养貂专业户　　　　　　　　2007年黑龙江双丰林场
　　Mink breeding family in the mountain　　2007 Shuangfeng Forest Plantation Heilongjiang

横道河子猫科野牲动物养虎人，为保护濒危东北虎，由当年8只现繁殖800多只　　2006年黑龙江横道河子
Tiger breeding at Hengdaohezi Feline center: to preserve the endangered Siberian tiger, the breeding program now has over 800 tigers from 8 heads at the beginning

68 五大连池冬季捕鱼人　　　　2005年黑龙江五大连池
Winter fishermen on the Lake Wudalian　2005 Wudalian Lake Heilongjiang

70 东乌旗蒙古人家 2007年内蒙吉东乌旗
Mongol family of the Dongwu banner 2007 Dongwu Banner Inner Mongolia

72 大山里骑马人 2007年黑龙讧双丰林场
Horsemen in the mountain 2007 Shuangfeng Forest Plantation Heilongjiang

74 雪乡人家 2005年黑龙江双丰林场
Snow country folk 2005 Shuangfeng Forest Plantation Heilongjiang

滑雪冠军从这里起飞 2007年黑龙江八一滑雪场
Ski champions start here 2007 August 1st Ski Station Heilongjiang

78 漠河老金沟淘金人　　　　2006年黑龙江漠河老金沟
   Gold diggers at the Mohe river　　2006 Mohe Laojingou

80 满族村养鹰人 2006年吉林韩屯
Falcon training in the Manchu village 2006 the Han clan hamlet Jilin

| 82 | 林海雪原的伐木工人 | 2005年黑龙江双丰林场 |
| | Timbermen in snow covered forest | 2005 Shuangfeng Forest Plantation Heilongjiang |

84 山村雪地上的马拉爬犁　　2007年黑龙江双丰林场
Horse drawn sledge in the snow　　2007 Shuangfeng Forest Plantation Heilongjiang

86 东北农村胶皮轮大马车　　　　　　　2006年吉林韩屯
Northeast farmer horse carriage with rubber tires　　2006 the Han clan hamlet Jilin

88 东北人喜爱二人转 "宁舍一顿饭 不舍二人转" 2007黑龙江双丰林场
Northeast people's favorite traditional pas-de-deux folk dance 2007 Jixi Heilongjiang

90 高寒禁区的裸体冬泳人　　　　　　　　2005年黑龙江齐齐哈尔
　　Winter swimmers from the restricted cold area　　2005 Tsitsihar Heilongjiang

Shooting "Northeast Men" with an 8x10 View Camera

In my life as a photographer, I am especially fond of traditional cameras and black-and-white photography. Having played with all sorts of 35mm, 120, 4×5 cameras, I even tried covering various photographic topics using different formats, so I can now say that I have the experience of each camera and each format's special sensation.

Facing the phenomenal development of digital photography, like a fortress being surrounded by a whole army, fewer and fewer people use traditional cameras. Maybe I am, after all, a stubborn conservative: I've always thought of digital photography as being too simple and not an interesting art. By the time I decided to practice traditional photography as far as I could, large format in Beijing circles became a hot item. I was caught in the excitement and without hesitation I acquired a Cambo Legend 8x10 monorail large-format view camera. Many of my friends were surprised: You're switching to landscape now? They asked me with consternation. No, I replied, I am going to shoot documentary portraits. Oh, documentary portraits? They remained skeptical. I knew perfectly how hard it was to do portraiture with a large format view camera, but precisely that difficulty was what motivated me to take up the challenge. At the same time, this decision strengthened my resolve to practice traditional photography up to its very limit.

In my enthusiasm I set up the view camera and then realized I overlooked another difficulty. Whose portrait was I going to shoot? My large circle of friends advised me again: You are in Beijing now, you should photograph the people in the hutong! Although I thought Beijing's hutong people had been overexploited, I gave it a try nevertheless, carrying my view camera around the Forbidden City and the Heaven's Temple, but could not find the feeling despite the effort. Then I realized: this land was not mine.

I am an authentic Northeast man; the Black Land (hei tudi) is the humus where I grew up. The mountains and rivers of this country of cockscomb shape are engraved in my heart. So I journeyed home with the 8×10 view camera on my back. Roaming the Heilongjiang river banks, braving the cold North wind and treading the thick snow, I ended up spending well over three winters there. It was a real homecoming; everything looked so familiar, and I was moved time after time by the stories of the Black Land. They touched me, astonished me. I can never forget them.

Those Oroqen* game hunters who live deep in the virgin forest far from modern civilization; and these Ewenki* reindeer people who refuse to descend from the mountain and to settle in the city; those Hoche* people who break ice to catch fish; and these one hundred thousand former career officers and soldiers who for the sake of developing the greater North wilderness, have sacrificed their youth, their whole life, and their descendants; those "zhiqing"- educated youth - from Shanghai and Beijing who were sent to this Black Land

and had never returned to their hometowns; and the five-month long frostless season that creates the so-called "natural refrigerator" in the artic restricted zone; and these hardy brave winter swimmers, etc., they were one after the other captured inside the box.

I could never forget the instant when through the frosted glass of the view finder I adjusted the focus to see sharply on the fully wrinkled face of the eighty-four-year-old aunt Li Fengyun, two lines of running tears that were telling me her past misery and suffering as a wartime comfort woman.

Equally touching was the roe deer breeding family at the Shuangfeng forest farm, forest workers Yan Fengping, husband and wife, who for four old hens received in exchange two wild fawns that had been caught in the mountains and bound for the kitchen slaughter. The couple would rather eat nothing and drink nothing, to save enough to feed the fawns with milk each day. They brought them to the hospital when they were sick, and took care of them and raised them as if they were their own children. Now the herd has grown to six or seven, playfully jumping around, really adorable. The old couple could not hide their joy when they watched their grandchildren play with the deer. Rich city folk who wanted game meat drove all the way to their house offering high price for the deer, still they refused to sell. The husband said: "the day I run out of money and food, I still will not sell them. Wait until I breed and raise more of them, then I will take them up the mountain and release them into the wild. The woods are where they belong."

Each household had its own story like this, and every time I made a portrait my heart and soul would be deeply affected. My eyes were often misty, sometimes I even forgot to press the shutter, forgot to remove the negative plate. It was in these moments of mixed emotions that my heart released the shutter of its own gate.

Large-format portraiture requires a calm and concentrated attitude. Because of the camera's tedious operation, every procedure and every link have to be exactly at their positions; the more anxious you are, the more mistakes you make. I happen to be all excited when I photograph, totally incapable of calmness. As anxiety strikes, either I overlook this or that, or I make mistake after mistake. Shooting with a large-format view camera, you have to be composed. Like a Buddhist monk, you need to cultivate your mind and your soul.

Large-format portraiture is very different from shooting with a small camera, which is easy to point-and-shoot, aiming for speed and reflex, instantaneous snapshots. With large-format, you need to think ahead before shooting. You need lots of pondering, documentation homework, feeding research materials into your notebook, drawing an itinerary on a map and following it, photographing one place after another, fully in control of your agenda. For instance photographing the Artic Village at the Mohe River, the gold diggers at Laojingou, or going to Station 18 by the Tarim River to photograph the Oroqen hunting tribe, reaching Fuyuan to shoot the Hoche fishermen, and so on, you need to follow the manual of procedures just like operating the view camera. You cannot run all over the place blindly.

Another requirement is about sentimental exchange. People from the Northeast are straightforward, they value loyalty and friendship. As long as you treat them with honest righteousness, they can dig their hearts out for you. Before I go to visit a family, if there are elders, I will usually buy some fruits, wine and cigarettes as presents. You need not rush in too soon, you should let some days pass and then befriend the family. After that they will let me shoot them in any way I like, especially after drinking to their content. When they stand in front of the view camera, they feel that they are being treated with respect. I want to thank my homeland folks, who are my elders and brothers and sisters, for their trust in me, for their understanding, their support and their willingness to let me photograph them. They need no promise nor any guarantee. They are just so happy when I give them the pictures taken of them.

Using large format for portraiture, I definitely prefer black-and-white to color. Black-and-white portraiture requires, first of all, good lighting. An overcast, cloudy day with diffuse light will add gentleness and gradation to the faces. On the contrary, bright weather days are to be avoided, as when light is strongest it exaggerates the contrast and reduces the sense of gradation. Under normal circumstances I use 200ASA film plus one notch of overexposure. During development I try to shorten the development time in order to weaken the contrast and reinforce the gradation in the parts in shade. Although this sounds good enough, when photographing people, given the excessively slow shutter speed, the final image is blurred if the subject moves even a little. Because the aperture cannot close up completely, the depth of field is insufficient; subjects ahead of and behind the focus zone are fuzzy. At an aperture of f32 the large format cannot be as good as an f5.6 of a small camera; hence with a short depth of field and a slow speed, it has always been rather difficult to do portraiture with a large format. If your eye is not sharp enough, your negative is wasted. In that way portraiture and landscape photography are two different things; there is an incremental degree of difficulty. When the picture is successfully taken, the striking power of a high-definition image and the charisma of the sharp details are not attainable by any small camera.

This series is my attempt to return to the original condition, a return to the truth. I have always wanted to revisit the earliest stage of photography, using the most simple, plot-free, no action no theme, to express purely black-and-white photography. Like counterpoint in music or silence at the climax of an opera, I want to reach the formless and soundless state that is the highest form of artistic expression.

Thanks to the large-format view camera, my frantic heart has now been calmed. It changed my thinking mode and my method of photography. From now on I can enjoy the charm and the infinite pleasure of large-format black-and-white photography.

Wang Fuchun
Harbin December 2008

+86 010-68871037   13161880003   wfc010@yahoo.com.cn

(*) Notes of the editor :
•Oroqen: ethnic minority in Inner Mongolia & Heilongjiang area, population less than 10,000 – mainly live off hunting.
•Ewenki: another minority in Inner Mongolia & Heilongjiang, population less than 30,000 – the only reindeer raising group in China.
•Hoche: an ethnic minority known for their fish-skin costume of Manchurian descent with a long fishing culture, mainly living in Heilongjiang.

我用8×10大画幅拍黑白《大东北》

在我的摄影生涯中,特别喜欢传统相机和黑白影像。135、120、4×5相机我都玩过了,而且用不同画幅的相机拍出不同题材的摄影专题,感受到了不同画幅相机给我带来的不同乐趣。

数码影像对传统影像的冲击,是科技发展的必然趋势,玩传统相机的人越来越少了。也许,我是个顽固派、保守派,总觉得数码拍片太容易。在我决心将传统影像传统到底时,正赶上北京大画幅悄然兴起,令我眼前一亮,兴奋不已。没有任何犹豫,买了一台金宝8×10单轨机。很多朋友好奇地问我,改拍风光了?我说:不,拍人物纪实!啊?拍人物纪实!朋友有点愕然和不解。我也深知拍大画幅人物的难度,但正是这个难度,我才去驾驭它。也许,是自我挑战,这也更加坚定了我坚持传统影像的决心。

兴奋过后,当我架上8×10大画幅相机,又生出一丝茫然感,茫然不知道拍什么人好。好多朋友说,你来北京了,去拍北京胡同吧!可我觉得北京胡同被人拍的太多了,我也试着背着8×10大相机在北京故宫、天坛转了一圈,愣是找不到感觉,这时我才意识到,这片土地并不属于我。

我是地地道道的东北人,黑土地是我成长的沃土,那鸡冠型版图上的山山水水,是我心中永远的牵挂。于是,我背上8×10重返黑土地,沿着黑龙江边境,迎着寒风,踏着积雪,历时三个冬天。真有一种回到家的感觉,看到什么都亲切,黑土地的故事一次次感染我,令我感动、惊奇、难忘。那远离现代文明深居原始森林的鄂伦春最后的狩猎人和不愿下山到城市定居的鄂温克驯鹿人;那开江捕鱼的赫哲人;为开发北大荒献了青春献终身,献了终身献子孙的十万转业官兵;融入黑土地没有返城的上海、北京知青;无霜期不足5个月,被称为高寒禁区的"天然冰箱"和勇敢的冬泳人等都被我一一收入镜中。

当我透过毛玻璃取景调焦时,看到84岁慰安妇李凤云老大妈那刻满苍桑的脸上,流淌着两行诉说她那段苦难人生岁月的眼泪,感慨万千。

更让我感动的是双丰林场的养狍子人家。老工人闫凤平夫妇,用四只老母鸡换回要吃肉的两只小野狍仔。老俩口舍不得吃,舍不得喝,每天给小狍子喂牛奶,病了去医院打针、吃药,像伺候自己孩子一样,把它们养大。如今繁殖六七只了,活蹦乱跳的,特别可爱。当看到小外孙和狍子一起嬉戏玩耍时,老两口就更开心了。好多城里有钱人要吃野味,开车到他家花2000元高价买他的狍子,他死活不卖。他说:我没有饭吃的那天,我也不会卖。等狍子繁殖多了,把它们放回大山去,大森林才是它们的家。

每一户人家,都有一个动人的故事,每拍一次我的心灵都被深深地感染和触动。我的眼睛是常常含泪模糊的,时常忘了拨插板、按快门……在情感交融中释放我心扉的快门。

用大画幅拍人物,要有平和的心态。因机器笨重操作繁琐,每一个程序和环节都得到位,你越急,越出错。我这个人拍片好激动,心总也静不下来,一着急,不是忘了这个,就是忘了那个,总是留有遗憾。拍大机器,求的是心静,如同出家人一样,炼的就是修心养性。

用大画幅拍人物，和小机器不一样。小机器举机就拍，求的是快速反映，瞬间抓取；大机器求稳重和准确的命中力。也就是说，想在前，拍在后，拍摄前要充分思考，做到心中有数。

拍8×10大画幅，黑白优于彩色，更具魅力。拍大画幅黑白，光照非常重要，最好是假阴天，散射光，人物面部影调柔和，层次丰富。最忌大晴天，光比越大，反差越大，暗部没有层次感。一般情况下200度胶片增加一挡曝光，冲洗时适当减少冲洗时间，这样减弱反差，暗部层次丰富。这样虽好，但拍人物快门速度过低，人物稍微一动就虚了。由于光圈收不到底，景深不够，前后人物会虚。大画幅F32，还不足小机器F5.6，所以景深小，速度慢，给大画幅拍人物带来难度。所以说，拍大画幅人物难于拍风光。如果真的成功了，那种高结像的影像冲击力和细节的魅力，是任何小机器无法比拟的。

拍大机器要讲感情交流。东北人实在，讲义气，重感情。只要你对他诚义，他会把心扒给你看。不能急着拍，得先跟他们交朋友，特别是喝酒喝到高兴时，怎么拍怎么是。他们站在大机器前那一双双明亮的眼睛真诚的对视着我，如同一尊尊活的雕塑屹立在我的面前，他们感到很自豪和有一种被尊重的感觉。他们那样信任我、理解我、支持我，我真的得感谢他们。

这是一次返朴归真的尝试，我总想回归到摄影术最初原始阶段，用无情节、无技巧、无动态的肖像式的大手笔手法，用最简单的也是最高的摄影艺术表现形式，达到大象无形，大巧若拙，大音希声的最高艺术境界。如同戏剧的高潮在于无声处；最美的音乐是无主题音乐；留有大片空白的中国画，意在给人以想象空间一样。

感谢大画幅相机，它迫使我燥动的心平静下来，改变了我的思维方式和拍摄方法，使我享受到了黑白影像的魅力和大画幅给我带来的无限乐趣。

2008年12月哈尔滨

编者注：
鄂伦春人：分散在黑龙江和内蒙古的少数民族，他们依靠狩猎为生。人口不到一万。
鄂温克人：分散在黑龙江和内蒙古的少数民族，中国唯一一个驯鹿的民族。人口不到三万。
赫哲人：住在黑龙江的满族后裔，有悠久的捕鱼文化。

王福春——简历

王福春，2002年从哈尔滨迁居北京，现在为自由摄影人。
拍有《火车上的中国人》、《中国蒸汽机车》、《黑土地》、《东北人家》、《大东北》、《东北虎》、《中国人的故事》等摄影专题。
第十七届全国影展金牌获得者，第三届中国摄影艺术金像奖得主，被中国摄影家协会授予"德艺双馨"优秀会员。

2000年《火车上的中国人》应邀参加丹麦奥胡斯IMAGE形象艺术摄影展馆大展。

2001年《火车上的中国人》在北京——福州45次列车中国摄影首开"北斗星"专列展出。

2002年《火车上的中国人》参加莫斯科摄影人之家国际摄影大展。

2002年《黑土地》参加第二届平遥国际摄影大展，《火车上的中国人》画册获中国优秀摄影师"阿尔卡特"大奖一等奖。

2003年《中国人的故事》参加第三届平遥国际摄影大展。

2004年《火车上的中国人》应法国邀请参加中法文化年"平遥在巴黎"展出。

2004年《东北人家》获第四届平遥国际摄影大展优秀摄影师大奖金奖。

2004年《火车上的中国人》参加紫禁城国际摄影大展。

2005年《火车与中国人》参加上海爱普生影艺坊摄影个展。

2005年《火车上的中国人》参加桂林首届国际摄影大展。

2005年《大东北》参加第五届平遥国际摄影大展。

2006年《中国蒸汽火车》参加第六届平遥国际摄影大展。

2006年《东北人》获山东济南当代国际摄影双年展最高学院大奖。

2006年《火车上的中国人》参加中国北京宋庄美术馆大展。

2006年《火车上的中国人》参加798百年印象画廊展。

2007年《黑土地》在哈尔滨哈药摄影国际摄影展馆展

2007年《地铁里的中国人》参加第七届平遥国际摄影大展

2008年《黑土地》获山东济南当代国际摄影双年展世界杰出职业摄影师奖。

2008年《天路藏人》参加第八届平遥国际摄影大展。

2009年《东北人》参加上海比极影像画廊个展。

Wang Fuchun - Resumé

Wang Fuchun is originally from Harbin. He moved to Beijing in 2002 as a freelance photographer
His major works include "Chinese on the Train", "The Steam Locomotives of China", "Black Land", "Northeast People", "The Greater Northeast", "Manchurian Tiger", "Chinese's Story" etc
Gold Medal winner of the 17th National Photo Exhibition, Oscar winner of the 3rd Chinese Art Photography, recipient of the outstanding membership of the Chinese Photographers' Association
Winner of the Alcatel Award for Best Photography Book "Chinese on the Train" in Pingyao in 2002 – Winner for "Northeast People" of the Best Contemporary Chinese Photographer award Pingyao 2004 - Winner with "Black Land" of the 2008 Outstanding Professional Photographer Award of the Jinan Photo Biennale

Exhibitions:

2000   "Chinese on the Train" in Denmark IMAGE festival

2001   "Chinese on the Train" exhibition on board of the Beijing-Fuzhou special   photo Train nb45

2002   "Chinese on the Train" at Moscow Photographers' House

2002   "Black Land" exhibition at Pingyao International Photo Festival

2003   "Chinese on the Train" at Pingyao International Photo Festival

2004   "Chinese on the Train" Paris group exhibition "Pingyao in Paris" and Beijing Forbidden City Photo Exhibition

2005   "Chinese on the Train" at Shanghai Epsite Gallery and at Guilin Photo Festival

2006   "Chinese on the Train" at Beijing Song Zhuang Art Museum and at 798 Photo Gallery

2007   "Chinese in the Subway" at Pingyao International Photo Festival

2007   "Black Land" at Harbin Hayao International Photo Exhibition Museum

2008   "Black Land" at the Jinan International Photo Biennale

2008   "Tibetans on the Heavenly Rairoad" at Pingyao International Photo Festival

2009   "Northeast Men" exhibition at Beaugeste Photo Gallery Shanghai

North East Men
Exhibition: 17th January - 28st February 2009

Photography: Wang Fuchun
Concept & design: Jean Loh \ Louisa Huang
Translation & editing: JL - Carole Jo Sharin - Xia Jingqing
Editor: beaugeste design solution shanghai
Publisher: Zhao Xiaoming
Published by: International Publishing House for China's Culture
2421 Pennsylvania Ave, N.W. Washington D.C. 20037-1718 USA
www.iphcc.org
ISBN 978-0-9814698-5-0
Printed in Shenzhen DXM Print
First edition: January 2009

Photography © Wang Fuchun
Copyright © 2009 beaugeste design solution shanghai for the book
All rights reserved

beaugeste photo gallery
lane 210 taikang road, building 5, studio 519, shanghai 200025, china
tel: 86-21 6466-9012   fax: 86-21 5465-3698-18
email: info@beaugeste-gallery.com
www.beaugeste-gallery.com

东北人
展期：2009年1月17日到2月28日

摄影：王福春
画册设计：尚陆、黄佳菁
翻译、校对：尚陆、Carole Jo Sharin、夏菁青
艺术总监与策展人：尚陆

编辑：上海比极广告设计有限公司
www.beaugestedesign.com

出版社：国际中国文化出版社
出版人：赵晓明
国际书号：ISBN 978-0-9814698-5-0

印刷：深圳德信美印刷有限公司
版次：2009年1月第一版

比极影像
上海市泰康路210弄5号楼519室
电话：86-21 6466-9012
传真：86-21 5465-3698*18

North East Men

Copyright © 2008 by beaugeste design solution Ltd

All rights reserved.
No part of this publication may be reproduced,
stored in a retrieval system, or transmitted in any form
or by any means, electronic, mechanical,
photocopying, recording ,or otherwise, without the
prior written permission of beaugeste design solution Ltd.

ISBN-13 : 978-0-9814698-5-0

Library of Congress Control Number:2008943566

International Publishing House for China's Culture
国 际 中 国 文 化 出 版 社
2421 Pennsylvania Ave, N.W. Washington D.C. 20037-1718
U.S.A.
http://www.iphcc.org

Printed in China on acid-free paper
First Printing: January 2009
10987654321

a book by beaugeste